Departmental Ditties & Other Verses by Rudyard Kipling

Rudyard Kipling: A great Victorian, a great writer of Empire, a great man.

Rudyard Kipling was one of the most popular writers of prose and poetry in the late 19th and 20th Century and awarded the Noble Prize for Literature in 1907.

Born in Bombay on 30th December 1865, as was the custom in those days, he and his sister were sent back to England when he was 5. The ill-treatment and cruelty by the couple who they boarded with in Portsmouth, Kipling himself suggested, contributed to the onset of his literary life. This was further enhanced by his return to India at age 16 to work on a local paper, as not only did this result in him writing constantly but also made him explore issues of identity and national allegiance which pervade much of his work.

Whilst he is best remembered for his classic children's stories and his popular poem 'If...' he is also regarded as a major innovator in the art of the short story.

Index of Contents

DEPARTMENTAL DITTIES

I have eaten your bread and salt,
  I have drunk your water and wine,
The deaths ye died I have watched beside,
  And the lives that ye led were mine.

Was there aught that I did not share
  In vigil or toil or ease,

One joy or woe that I did not know,
　　Dear hearts across the seas?

I have written the tale of our life
　　For a sheltered people's mirth,
In jesting guise—but ye are wise,
And ye know what the jest is worth.

GENERAL SUMMARY

We are very slightly changed
From the semi-apes who ranged
　　India's prehistoric clay;
Whoso drew the longest bow,
Ran his brother down, you know,
　　As we run men down today.

"Dowb," the first of all his race,
Met the Mammoth face to face
　　On the lake or in the cave,
Stole the steadiest canoe,
Ate the quarry others slew,
　　Died—and took the finest grave.

When they scratched the reindeer-bone
Someone made the sketch his own,
　　Filched it from the artist—then,
Even in those early days,
Won a simple Viceroy's praise
　　Through the toil of other men.

Ere they hewed the Sphinx's visage
Favoritism governed kissage,
Even as it does in this age.

Who shall doubt the secret hid
Under Cheops' pyramid
Was that the contractor did
　　Cheops out of several millions?
Or that Joseph's sudden rise
To Comptroller of Supplies
Was a fraud of monstrous size
　　On King Pharoah's swart Civilians?

Thus, the artless songs I sing
Do not deal with anything

New or never said before.

As it was in the beginning,
Is today official sinning,
    And shall be forevermore.

ARMY HEADQUARTERS

Old is the song that I sing—
    Old as my unpaid bills—
Old as the chicken that kitmutgars bring
Men at dak-bungalows—old as the Hills.

Ahasuerus Jenkins of the "Operatic Own"
    Was dowered with a tenor voice of super-Santley tone.

His views on equitation were, perhaps, a trifle queer;
He had no seat worth mentioning, but oh! he had an ear.

He clubbed his wretched company a dozen times a day,
He used to quit his charger in a parabolic way,
His method of saluting was the joy of all beholders,
But Ahasuerus Jenkins had a head upon his shoulders.

He took two months to Simla when the year was at the spring,
And underneath the deodars eternally did sing.

He warbled like a bulbul, but particularly at
Cornelia Agrippina who was musical and fat.

She controlled a humble husband, who, in turn, controlled a Dept.,
Where Cornelia Agrippina's human singing-birds were kept
From April to October on a plump retaining fee,
Supplied, of course, per mensem, by the Indian Treasury.

Cornelia used to sing with him, and Jenkins used to play;
He praised unblushingly her notes, for he was false as they:
So when the winds of April turned the budding roses brown,
Cornelia told her husband: "Tom, you mustn't send him down."

They haled him from his regiment which didn't much regret him;
They found for him an office-stool, and on that stool they set him,
To play with maps and catalogues three idle hours a day,
And draw his plump retaining fee—which means his double pay.

Now, ever after dinner, when the coffeecups are brought,

Ahasuerus waileth o'er the grand pianoforte;
And, thanks to fair Cornelia, his fame hath waxen great,
And Ahasuerus Jenkins is a power in the State.

STUDY OF AN ELEVATION, IN INDIAN INK

This ditty is a string of lies.
But—how the deuce did Gubbins rise?

POTIPHAR GUBBINS, C. E.,

Stands at the top of the tree;
And I muse in my bed on the reasons that led
To the hoisting of Potiphar G.

Potiphar Gubbins, C. E.,
Is seven years junior to Me;
Each bridge that he makes he either buckles or breaks,
And his work is as rough as he.

Potiphar Gubbins, C. E.,
Is coarse as a chimpanzee;
And I can't understand why you gave him your hand,
Lovely Mehitabel Lee.

Potiphar Gubbins, C. E.,
Is dear to the Powers that Be;
For They bow and They smile in an affable style
Which is seldom accorded to Me.

Potiphar Gubbins, C. E.,
Is certain as certain can be
Of a highly-paid post which is claimed by a host
Of seniors—including Me.

Careless and lazy is he,
Greatly inferior to Me.

What is the spell that you manage so well,
Commonplace Potiphar G.?

Lovely Mehitabel Lee,
Let me inquire of thee,
Should I have riz to what Potiphar is,
Hadst thou been mated to me?

A LEGEND

This is the reason why Rustum Beg,
Rajah of Kolazai,
Drinketh the "simpkin" and brandy peg,
Maketh the money to fly,
Vexeth a Government, tender and kind,
Also—but this is a detail—blind.

RUSTUM BEG of Kolazai—slightly backward native state
Lusted for a C. S. I.,—so began to sanitate.
Built a Jail and Hospital—nearly built a City drain—
Till his faithful subjects all thought their Ruler was insane.

Strange departures made he then—yea, Departments stranger still,
Half a dozen Englishmen helped the Rajah with a will,
Talked of noble aims and high, hinted of a future fine
For the state of Kolazai, on a strictly Western line.

Rajah Rustum held his peace; lowered octroi dues a half;
Organized a State Police; purified the Civil Staff;
Settled cess and tax afresh in a very liberal way;
Cut temptations of the flesh—also cut the Bukhshi's pay;

Roused his Secretariat to a fine Mahratta fury,
By a Hookum hinting at supervision of dasturi;
Turned the State of Kolazai very nearly upside-down;
When the end of May was nigh, waited his achievement crown.

When the Birthday Honors came,
Sad to state and sad to see,
Stood against the Rajah's name nothing more than C. I. E.!

Things were lively for a week in the State of Kolazai.
Even now the people speak of that time regretfully.

How he disendowed the Jail—stopped at once the City drain;
Turned to beauty fair and frail—got his senses back again;
Doubled taxes, cesses, all; cleared away each new-built thana;
Turned the two-lakh Hospital into a superb Zenana;

Heaped upon the Bukhshi Sahib wealth and honors manifold;
Clad himself in Eastern garb—squeezed his people as of old.

Happy, happy Kolazai! Never more will Rustum Beg
Play to catch the Viceroy's eye. He prefers the "simpkin" peg.

"Now there were two men in one city;
the one rich and the other poor."

Jack Barrett went to Quetta
  Because they told him to.
He left his wife at Simla
  On three-fourths his monthly screw:
Jack Barrett died at Quetta
  Ere the next month's pay he drew.

Jack Barrett went to Quetta.
  He didn't understand
The reason of his transfer
  From the pleasant mountain-land:
The season was September,
  And it killed him out of hand.

Jack Barrett went to Quetta,
  And there gave up the ghost,
Attempting two men's duty
  In that very healthy post;
And Mrs. Barrett mourned for him
  Five lively months at most.

Jack Barrett's bones at Quetta
  Enjoy profound repose;
But I shouldn't be astonished
  If now his spirit knows
The reason of his transfer
  From the Himalayan snows.

And, when the Last Great Bugle Call
  Adown the Hurnal throbs,
When the last grim joke is entered
  In the big black Book of Jobs,
And Quetta graveyards give again
  Their victims to the air,
I shouldn't like to be the man
  Who sent Jack Barrett there.

THE POST THAT FITTED

Though tangled and twisted the course of true love
    This ditty explains,
No tangle's so tangled it cannot improve
    If the Lover has brains.

Ere the steamer bore him Eastward, Sleary was engaged to marry
An attractive girl at Tunbridge, whom he called "my little Carrie."

Sleary's pay was very modest; Sleary was the other way.
Who can cook a two-plate dinner on eight poor rupees a day?

Long he pondered o'er the question in his scantly furnished quarters—
Then proposed to Minnie Boffkin, eldest of Judge Boffkin's daughters.

Certainly an impecunious Subaltern was not a catch,
But the Boffkins knew that Minnie mightn't make another match.

So they recognised the business and, to feed and clothe the bride,
Got him made a Something Something somewhere on the Bombay side.

Anyhow, the billet carried pay enough for him to marry—
As the artless Sleary put it:—"Just the thing for me and Carrie."

Did he, therefore, jilt Miss Boffkin—impulse of a baser mind?
No! He started epileptic fits of an appalling kind.

[Of his modus operandi only this much I could gather:—
"Pears's shaving sticks will give you little taste and lots of lather."]

Frequently in public places his affliction used to smite
Sleary with distressing vigour—always in the Boffkins' sight.

Ere a week was over Minnie weepingly returned his ring,
Told him his "unhappy weakness" stopped all thought of marrying.

Sleary bore the information with a chastened holy joy,—
Epileptic fits don't matter in Political employ,—

Wired three short words to Carrie—took his ticket, packed his kit—
Bade farewell to Minnie Boffkin in one last, long, lingering fit.

Four weeks later, Carrie Sleary read—and laughed until she wept—
Mrs. Boffkin's warning letter on the "wretched epilept"...

Year by year, in pious patience, vengeful Mrs. Boffkin sits
Waiting for the Sleary babies to develop Sleary's fits.

Walpole talks of "a man and his price."
    List to a ditty queer—
The sale of a Deputy-Acting-Vice-
    Resident-Engineer,
Bought like a bullock, hoof and hide,
By the Little Tin Gods on the Mountain Side.

By the Laws of the Family Circle 'tis written in letters of brass
That only a Colonel from Chatham can manage the Railways of State,
Because of the gold on his breeks, and the subjects wherein he must pass;
Because in all matters that deal not with Railways his knowledge is great.

Now Exeter Battleby Tring had laboured from boyhood to eld
On the Lines of the East and the West, and eke of the North and South;
Many Lines had he built and surveyed—important the posts which he held;
And the Lords of the Iron Horse were dumb when he opened his mouth.

Black as the raven his garb, and his heresies jettier still—
Hinting that Railways required lifetimes of study and knowledge—
Never clanked sword by his side—Vauban he knew not nor drill—
Nor was his name on the list of the men who had passed through the "College."

Wherefore the Little Tin Gods harried their little tin souls,
Seeing he came not from Chatham, jingled no spurs at his heels,
Knowing that, nevertheless, was he first on the Government rolls
For the billet of "Railway Instructor to Little Tin Gods on Wheels."

Letters not seldom they wrote him, "having the honour to state,"
It would be better for all men if he were laid on the shelf.
Much would accrue to his bank-book, an he consented to wait
Until the Little Tin Gods built him a berth for himself,

"Special, well paid, and exempt from the Law of the Fifty and Five,
Even to Ninety and Nine"—these were the terms of the pact:
Thus did the Little Tin Gods (long may Their Highnesses thrive!)
Silence his mouth with rupees, keeping their Circle intact;

Appointing a Colonel from Chatham who managed the Bhamo State Line
(The which was one mile and one furlong—a guaranteed twenty-inch gauge),
So Exeter Battleby Tring consented his claims to resign,
And died, on four thousand a month, in the ninetieth year of his age!

We have another viceroy now,—those days are dead and done
Of Delilah Aberyswith and depraved Ulysses Gunne.

Delilah Aberyswith was a lady—not too young—
With a perfect taste in dresses and a badly-bitted tongue,
With a thirst for information, and a greater thirst for praise,
And a little house in Simla in the Prehistoric Days.

By reason of her marriage to a gentleman in power,
Delilah was acquainted with the gossip of the hour;
And many little secrets, of the half-official kind,
Were whispered to Delilah, and she bore them all in mind.

She patronized extensively a man, Ulysses Gunne,
Whose mode of earning money was a low and shameful one.
He wrote for certain papers, which, as everybody knows,
Is worse than serving in a shop or scaring off the crows.

He praised her "queenly beauty" first; and, later on, he hinted
At the "vastness of her intellect" with compliment unstinted.
He went with her a-riding, and his love for her was such
That he lent her all his horses and—she galled them very much.

One day, THEY brewed a secret of a fine financial sort;
It related to Appointments, to a Man and a Report.
'Twas almost worth the keeping,—only seven people knew it—
And Gunne rose up to seek the truth and patiently pursue it.

It was a Viceroy's Secret, but—perhaps the wine was red—
Perhaps an Aged Councillor had lost his aged head—
Perhaps Delilah's eyes were bright—Delilah's whispers sweet—
The Aged Member told her what 'twere treason to repeat.

Ulysses went a-riding, and they talked of love and flowers;
Ulysses went a-calling, and he called for several hours;
Ulysses went a-waltzing, and Delilah helped him dance—
Ulysses let the waltzes go, and waited for his chance.

The summer sun was setting, and the summer air was still,
The couple went a-walking in the shade of Summer Hill.
The wasteful sunset faded out in Turkish-green and gold,
Ulysses pleaded softly, and— that bad Delilah told!

Next morn, a startled Empire learnt the all-important news;
Next week, the Aged Councillor was shaking in his shoes.
Next month, I met Delilah and she did not show the least

Hesitation in affirming that Ulysses was a "beast."

We have another Viceroy now, those days are dead and done—
Of Delilah Aberyswith and most mean Ulysses Gunne!

Hurree Chunder Mookerjee, pride of Bow Bazaar,
Owner of a native press, "Barrishter-at-Lar,"
 Waited on the Government with a claim to wear
Sabres by the bucketful, rifles by the pair.

Then the Indian Government winked a wicked wink,
Said to Chunder Mookerjee: "Stick to pen and ink.
They are safer implements, but, if you insist,
We will let you carry arms wheresoe'er you list."

Hurree Chunder Mookerjee sought the gunsmith and
Bought the tubes of Lancaster, Ballard, Dean, and Bland,
Bought a shiny bowie-knife, bought a town-made sword,
Jingled like a carriage-horse when he went abroad.

But the Indian Government, always keen to please,
Also gave permission to horrid men like these—
Yar Mahommed Yusufzai, down to kill or steal,
Chimbu Singh from Bikaneer, Tantia the Bhil;

Killar Khan the Marri chief, Jowar Singh the Sikh,
Nubbee Baksh Punjabi Jat, Abdul Huq Rafiq—
He was a Wahabi; last, little Boh Hla-oo
Took advantage of the Act—took a Snider too.

They were unenlightened men, Ballard knew them not.
They procured their swords and guns chiefly on the spot;
And the lore of centuries, plus a hundred fights,
Made them slow to disregard one another's rights.

With a unanimity dear to patriot hearts
All those hairy gentlemen out of foreign parts
Said: "The good old days are back—let us go to war!"
 Swaggered down the Grand Trunk Road into Bow Bazaar,

Nubbee Baksh Punjabi Jat found a hide-bound flail;
Chimbu Singh from Bikaneer oiled his Tonk jezail;
Yar Mahommed Yusufzai spat and grinned with glee
As he ground the butcher-knife of the Khyberee.

Jowar Singh the Sikh procured sabre, quoit, and mace,
Abdul Huq, Wahabi, jerked his dagger from its place,
While amid the jungle-grass danced and grinned and jabbered
Little Boh Hla-oo and cleared his dah-blade from the scabbard.

What became of Mookerjee? Soothly, who can say?
Yar Mahommed only grins in a nasty way,
Jowar Singh is reticent, Chimbu Singh is mute.
But the belts of all of them simply bulge with loot.

What became of Ballard's guns? Afghans black and grubby
Sell them for their silver weight to the men of Pubbi;
And the shiny bowie-knife and the town-made sword are
Hanging in a Marri camp just across the Border.

What became of Mookerjee? Ask Mahommed Yar
Prodding Siva's sacred bull down the Bow Bazaar.
Speak to placid Nubbee Baksh—question land and sea—
Ask the Indian Congressmen—only don't ask me!

PINK DOMINOES

"They are fools who kiss and tell"—
  Wisely has the poet sung.
Man may hold all sorts of posts
  If he'll only hold his tongue.

Jenny and Me were engaged, you see,
  On the eve of the Fancy Ball;
So a kiss or two was nothing to you
  Or any one else at all.

Jenny would go in a domino—
  Pretty and pink but warm;
While I attended, clad in a splendid
  Austrian uniform.

Now we had arranged, through notes exchanged
  Early that afternoon,
At Number Four to waltz no more,
  But to sit in the dusk and spoon.

I wish you to see that Jenny and Me
  Had barely exchanged our troth;
So a kiss or two was strictly due

By, from, and between us both.

When Three was over, an eager lover,
  I fled to the gloom outside;
And a Domino came out also
  Whom I took for my future bride.

That is to say, in a casual way,
  I slipped my arm around her;
With a kiss or two (which is nothing to you),
  And ready to kiss I found her.

She turned her head and the name she said
  Was certainly not my own;
But ere I could speak, with a smothered shriek
  She fled and left me alone.

Then Jenny came, and I saw with shame
  She'd doffed her domino;
And I had embraced an alien waist—
  But I did not tell her so.

Next morn I knew that there were two
  Dominoes pink, and one
Had cloaked the spouse of Sir Julian House,
  Our big Political gun.

Sir J. was old, and her hair was gold,
  And her eye was a blue cerulean;
And the name she said when she turned her head
  Was not in the least like "Julian."

THE MAN WHO COULD WRITE

Shun—shun the Bowl! That fatal, facile drink
  Has ruined many geese who dipped their quills in 't;
Bribe, murder, marry, but steer clear of Ink
  Save when you write receipts for paid-up bills in 't.

There may be silver in the "blue-black"—all
I know of is the iron and the gall.

Boanerges Blitzen, servant of the Queen,
Is a dismal failure—is a Might-have-been.
In a luckless moment he discovered men
Rise to high position through a ready pen.

Boanerges Blitzen argued therefore—"I,
With the selfsame weapon, can attain as high."
Only he did not possess when he made the trial,
Wicked wit of C-lv-n, irony of L—l.

[Men who spar with Government need, to back their blows,
Something more than ordinary journalistic prose.]

Never young Civilian's prospects were so bright,
Till an Indian paper found that he could write:
Never young Civilian's prospects were so dark,
When the wretched Blitzen wrote to make his mark.
Certainly he scored it, bold, and black, and firm,
In that Indian paper—made his seniors squirm,
Quoted office scandals, wrote the tactless truth—
Was there ever known a more misguided youth?
When the Rag he wrote for praised his plucky game,
Boanerges Blitzen felt that this was Fame;
When the men he wrote of shook their heads and swore,
Boanerges Blitzen only wrote the more:

Posed as Young Ithuriel, resolute and grim,
Till he found promotion didn't come to him;
Till he found that reprimands weekly were his lot,
And his many Districts curiously hot.

Till he found his furlough strangely hard to win,
Boanerges Blitzen didn't care to pin:
Then it seemed to dawn on him something wasn't right—
Boanerges Blitzen put it down to "spite";

Languished in a District desolate and dry;
Watched the Local Government yearly pass him by;
Wondered where the hitch was; called it most unfair.

That was seven years ago—and he still is there!

MUNICIPAL

"Why is my District death-rate low?"
  Said Binks of Hezabad.
"Well, drains, and sewage-outfalls are
  "My own peculiar fad.

"I learnt a lesson once, It ran
"Thus," quoth that most veracious man:—

It was an August evening and, in snowy garments clad,
I paid a round of visits in the lines of Hezabad;
When, presently, my Waler saw, and did not like at all,
A Commissariat elephant careering down the Mall.

I couldn't see the driver, and across my mind it rushed
That that Commissariat elephant had suddenly gone musth.

I didn't care to meet him, and I couldn't well get down,
So I let the Waler have it, and we headed for the town.

The buggy was a new one and, praise Dykes, it stood the strain,
Till the Waler jumped a bullock just above the City Drain;
And the next that I remember was a hurricane of squeals,
And the creature making toothpicks of my five-foot patent wheels.

He seemed to want the owner, so I fled, distraught with fear,
To the Main Drain sewage-outfall while he snorted in my ear—
Reached the four-foot drain-head safely and, in darkness and despair,
Felt the brute's proboscis fingering my terror-stiffened hair.

Heard it trumpet on my shoulder—tried to crawl a little higher—
Found the Main Drain sewage outfall blocked, some eight feet up, with mire;
And, for twenty reeking minutes, Sir, my very marrow froze,
While the trunk was feeling blindly for a purchase on my toes!

It missed me by a fraction, but my hair was turning grey
Before they called the drivers up and dragged the brute away.

Then I sought the City Elders, and my words were very plain.
They flushed that four-foot drain-head and—it never choked again!

You may hold with surface-drainage, and the sun-for-garbage cure,
Till you've been a periwinkle shrinking coyly up a sewer.

I believe in well-flushed culverts....

                    This is why the death-rate's small;
And, if you don't believe me, get shikarred yourself. That's all.

A CODE OF MORALS

        Lest you should think this story true
        I merely mention I
        Evolved it lately. 'Tis a most

Unmitigated misstatement.

Now Jones had left his new-wed bride to keep his house in order,
And hied away to the Hurrum Hills above the Afghan border,
To sit on a rock with a heliograph; but ere he left he taught
His wife the working of the Code that sets the miles at naught.

And Love had made him very sage, as Nature made her fair;
So Cupid and Apollo linked, per heliograph, the pair.
At dawn, across the Hurrum Hills, he flashed her counsel wise—
At e'en, the dying sunset bore her husband's homilies.

He warned her 'gainst seductive youths in scarlet clad and gold,
As much as 'gainst the blandishments paternal of the old;
But kept his gravest warnings for (hereby the ditty hangs)
That snowy-haired Lothario, Lieutenant-General Bangs.

'Twas General Bangs, with Aide and Staff, who tittupped on the way,
When they beheld a heliograph tempestuously at play.
They thought of Border risings, and of stations sacked and burnt—
So stopped to take the message down—and this is what they learnt—

"Dash dot dot, dot, dot dash, dot dash dot" twice. The General swore.

"Was ever General Officer addressed as 'dear' before?
"'My Love,' i' faith! 'My Duck,' Gadzooks! 'My darling popsy-wop!'
"Spirit of great Lord Wolseley, who is on that mountaintop?"

The artless Aide-de-camp was mute; the gilded Staff were still,
As, dumb with pent-up mirth, they booked that message from the hill;
For clear as summer lightning-flare, the husband's warning ran:—
"Don't dance or ride with General Bangs—a most immoral man."

[At dawn, across the Hurrum Hills, he flashed her counsel wise—
But, howsoever Love be blind, the world at large hath eyes.]
With damnatory dot and dash he heliographed his wife
Some interesting details of the General's private life.

The artless Aide-de-camp was mute, the shining Staff were still,
And red and ever redder grew the General's shaven gill.

And this is what he said at last (his feelings matter not):—
"I think we've tapped a private line. Hi! Threes about there! Trot!"

All honour unto Bangs, for ne'er did Jones thereafter know
By word or act official who read off that helio.

But the tale is on the Frontier, and from Michni to Mooltan

They know the worthy General as "that most immoral man."

THE LAST DEPARTMENT

Twelve hundred million men are spread
 About this Earth, and I and You
Wonder, when You and I are dead,
 "What will those luckless millions do?"

None whole or clean," we cry, "or free from stain
Of favour." Wait awhile, till we attain
 The Last Department where nor fraud nor fools,
Nor grade nor greed, shall trouble us again.

Fear, Favour, or Affection—what are these
To the grim Head who claims our services?
 I never knew a wife or interest yet
Delay that pukka step, miscalled "decease";

When leave, long overdue, none can deny;
When idleness of all Eternity
 Becomes our furlough, and the marigold
Our thriftless, bullion-minting Treasury

Transferred to the Eternal Settlement,
Each in his strait, wood-scantled office pent,
 No longer Brown reverses Smith's appeals,
Or Jones records his Minute of Dissent.

And One, long since a pillar of the Court,
As mud between the beams thereof is wrought;
 And One who wrote on phosphates for the crops
Is subject-matter of his own Report.

These be the glorious ends whereto we pass—
Let Him who Is, go call on Him who Was;
 And He shall see the mallie steals the slab
For currie-grinder, and for goats the grass.

A breath of wind, a Border bullet's flight,
A draught of water, or a horse's fright—
 The droning of the fat Sheristadar
Ceases, the punkah stops, and falls the night

For you or Me. Do those who live decline
The step that offers, or their work resign?

Trust me, Today's Most Indispensables,
Five hundred men can take your place or mine.

Rudyard Kipling – A Short Biography

Born in Bombay on 30th December 1865, Joseph Rudyard Kipling wrote short stories, poems and novels, a body of work whose reputation is in constant flux as his presentations and interpretations of empire are viewed within the changing context of empirical absolution in the twentieth century. Having spent the first five years of his life in India he felt a natural affinity for the country, though his upbringing had a distinctly colonial taste flavour. He was born in the Bombay Presidency of British India to Lockwood Kipling, an English art teacher and illustrator who took a position as professor of architectural sculpture in the Jeejeebhoy School of Art and Alice MacDonald, spoken of by the a Viceroy of India that "dullness and Mrs Kipling cannot exist in the same room". Though their presence in India was principally artistic and educational, rather than political, the company they kept and the establishments in which they kept it indicate an existence very much benefitting from the British Empire. Lockwood would later go on to assume a position as curator of the Lahore Museum, while working on various illustrations for Rudyard's writing, and various decorations for the Victoria and Albert museum in London. Much of his work, then, was coloured by the empire, whether in service to or benefitting from, and it was into this distinctly British experience of India that Rudyard was born.

Lockwood and Alice had met and fallen in love at Rudyard Lake in Rudyard, Staffordshire, and their affections for the area were so great they chose to refer to the lake in naming their first-born. Alice came from a family of four sisters, all of whose marriages were significant and well-arranged; moreover, Rudyard's most famous relative was Stanley Baldwin, Conservative Prime Minister on three occasions in the 1920s and 1930s. Kipling's sense of belonging in Bombay is found in 'To the City of Bombay' in the dedication to Seven Seas, a collection of poems published in 1900, which reads:—

> Mother of Cities to me,
> For I was born in her gate,
> Between the palms and the sea,
> Where the world-end steamers wait.

His parents considered themselves Anglo-Indians, and he would later assume this classification although he did not live there long. His first five years, which he describes as days of "strong light and darkness", ended when he and his three-year-old sister Alice were removed to Southsea, Plymouth, to board with Captain Pryse Agar Holloway and his wife Mrs Sarah Holloway, a couple who cared for the children of couples born in British India. They were there for six years and Kipling would later recall their time there with horror, describing incidents of cruelty and neglect and wondering whether it was these which speeded up his literary maturity, for "it made me give attention to the lies I soon found it necessary to tell: and this, I presume, is the foundation of literary effort".

Alice's time, by contrast, was relatively comfortable, Mrs Holloway hoping that she would marry her son, though this ambition would not come to fruition. They did have relatives in England, a maternal aunt Georgiana and her husband who lived in Fulham, London, in a house at which they spent a month each Christmas and which Kipling later described as "a paradise which I verily believe saved me". Their mother returned in 1877 and removed them from their custody with the Holloways. A year later he gained admission to the United Services College at Westward Ho! in Devon, a recently established school with the intention of readying boys for military service in the British Army. His time here was fraught physically, though emotionally it proved fruitful for he began several firm friendships with other boys at the school. Moreover, he found in it inspiration for the setting of his series of schoolboy stories, Stalky and Co, begun in 1899. Meanwhile, his sister Alice had returned to Southsea and was boarding with Florence Garrard, with whom he fell in love and on whom he modeled Maisie in his first novel, The Light That Failed, published in 1891. At sixteen he was found lacking in the academic perspicacity necessary to undertake a scholarship to Oxford University, his parents meanwhile lacking the wherewithal to finance him therein. As such his father sought a job for him in Lahore, Punjab, where he was now a museum curator. The position he found for his son was as assistant editor of the Civil and Military Gazette, a small local newspaper. Kipling left for India on 20th September 1882, arriving in Bombay on 18th October. "There were yet three or four days" rail to Lahore, where my people lived. After these, my English years fell away, nor ever, I think, came back in full strength".

The Gazette appeared six days of the week, year-round save for a short break at both Christmas and Easter. Its editor Stephen Wheeler was diligent but Kipling's writing was insatiable, and he came to consider the paper his "mistress and most true love". In the summer of 1883 Kipling visited Shimla, the colonial hill-station and summer capital of British India which was then called Simla. Chosen by the British owing to its resemblance of English climate and scenery (as far as was possible in India), it became the seat of the Viceroy of India for the six months on the plains which were too hot for the British temperament, and subsequently became a "centre of power as well as pleasure". Lockwood was asked to serve in the Church there, and his family became yearly visitors while Kipling himself would take his annual leave here from 1885-88. The value of this time is evident from the regularity with which Simla appears in his writing for the Gazette, which in his journals he describes the time as

> "....pure joy—every golden hour counted. It began in heat and discomfort, by rail and road. It ended in the cool evening, with a wood fire in one's bedroom, and next morn—thirty more of them ahead!—the early cup of tea, the Mother who brought it in, and the long talks of us all together again."

In 1886, his Departmental Ditties appeared, his first collection of verse, and brought with it a change of editor; Kay Robinson, Wheeler's replacement, was in favour of Kipling's creativity and granted him more freedom in that respect, even asking him to write short stories to appear in the newspaper. The vivacity of his writing was captured in a description of him by an ex-colleague at the Gazette, saying he "never knew such a fellow for ink—he simply revelled in it, filling up his pen viciously, and then throwing the contents all over the office, so that it was almost dangerous to approach him". While in Lahore, he had thirty-nine stories published in the Gazette between November 1886 and June 1887. Most of these are compiled in Plain Tales from the Hills, his first collection of prose, which was published in January 1888 in Calcutta, shortly after his 22nd birthday. In November 1887, he transferred from the Gazette to its much larger sister newspaper, The Pioneer, based in Allahabad. The pace of his writing remained, and in 1888 he published six collections of stories, Soldiers Three, The Story of the Gadsbys, In Black and White, Under the Deodars, The Phantom Rickshaw and Wee Willie Winkie, composed of some 41 stories. In addition, his position as The Pioneer's special correspondent in the Western region of Rajputna, he wrote many sketches which were later compiled in Letters of Marque and published in From Sea to Sea and Other Sketches, Letters of Travel.

A dispute in 1889 saw him discharged from The Pioneer, though by now he had been considering his future and sold the rights to his six volumes of stories for £200 and a small royalty, while the Plain Tales fetched £50, along with six months' salary from The Pioneer in lieu of notice. Using the money to undertake a pilgrimage to London, the literary centre of the British Empire, he left India on 9th March 1889, travelling via Rangoon, San Francisco, Hong Kong and Japan, then through the United States writing articles for The Pioneer which were also included in From Sea to Sea and Other Sketches, Letters of Travel. Arriving in England at Liverpool on October 1889, London and his literary début there beckoned.

His first task was to find a place to live, and he eventually settled on quarters in Villiers Street, Strand. The next two years saw several stories accepted by various magazine editors, the publication of the novel The Light That Failed, a nervous breakdown, the collaboration with Wolcott Balestier on the novel (uncharacterstically misspelt) The Naulhaka, and in 1891, following his doctors' advice, he embarked on a further sea voyage, travelling to South Africa, Australia, New Zealand and also returning to India. His plans to spend Christmas with his family were cut short on the news of Balestier's sudden death from typhoid fever, prompting an immediate return to London. Before he left, he had proposed to Balestier's sister Caroline Starr Balestier, with whom he had been having a hushed romance for just over a year. Back in London, Life's Handicap was published in 1891, a collection of short stories whose subject was the British in India, and British India. On 18th January 1892 aged 26 he married Caroline in the midst of an epidemic of influenza. Caroline was given away by Henry James, the famous and celebrated American author.

Honeymooning in Japan, they travelled via Vermont, America, to visit the Balestier estate, and upon arrival in Yokahama they found that their bank, The New Oriental Banking Corporation, had failed, though this loss did not deter them and they returned to Vermont, Caroline now pregnant with their first child. Renting a cottage on a farm for $10 per month, they lived a spartan existence and were "extraordinarily and self-centredly content". The named the residence Bliss Cottage, and it was here that the child was born, named Josephine, "in three foot of snow on the night of 29th December 1892. Her Mother's birthday being the 31st and mine the 30th we congratulated her on her sense of the fitness of things." While here, Kipling had his first ideas for the Jungle Books. Shortly after Josephine was born the couple moved in pursuit of more space and comfort, buying ten acres overlooking the Connecticut River from Caroline's brother. The house they built there was inspired by the Mughul architecture he encountered in Lahore, and was named Naulakha (this time correctly spelt) in honour of Wolcott. His literary output in four years here included the Jungle Books, a collection of short stories entitled The Day's Work, the novel Captain Courageous and a plethora of poetry, of which most notably the volume The Seven Seas and his Barrack-Room Ballads. Meanwhile, he enjoyed correspondence with the many children who wrote to him about the Jungle Books.

In between this writing, Kipling took regular visitors. Most notably Arthur Conan Doyle came, bringing golf clubs and staying for two days to give Kipling an extended golf lesson. Kipling enjoyed the game so much that he continued to play, even in winter with special red balls, though he found that the ice would lead to drives travelling two miles as they slid "down the long slope to the Connecticut River". Elsie, the couple's second daughter, was born in February 1896, and by this time it is thought that their marriage had lost its original spark of spontaneity and descended into routine, though they remained loyal to one another. By now, failed arbitration between the United States and England over a border dispute involving British Guiana incited Anglo-American tensions which, in May 1896, resulted in a confrontation between Kipling and Caroline's brother, resulting in his arrest and, in the hearing which followed, the destruction of Kipling's private life, leaving him exhausted and miserable and leading to their return to England.

They had settled Torquay, Devon, by September 1896, and he remained socially present and literarily productive. The success of his writing had brought him fame, and he had responded with a sense of duty to include in his writing elements of political persuasion, most notably in his two poems Recessional and The White Man's Burden, which caused controversy when they were published in 1897 and 1899 respectively. Many considered them anthemic to the empire, propaganda for the imperial mindset so prevalent in the Victoria era. Their first son, John, was born in August 1887. Another journey to South Africa began a tradition of wintering there, which continued until 1908. His reputation as Poet of the Empire saw him well-received by politicians in the Cape Colony, and he started the newspaper The Friend for Lord Roberts and the British troops in Bloemfontein. Back in England, they moved to Rottingdean, East Sussex, in 1897, and in 1902 he bought Bateman's, a house built in 1630, which was his home from until his death in 1936. Kim was published in 1902, after which he collected material for Just So Stories for Little Children, published a year later. Both he and Josephine developed pneumonia while visiting the United States, from which she later died.

This decade proved his most successful, being awarded the Nobel Prize for Literature in 1907, the prize citation reading "in consideration of the power of observation, originality of imagination, virility of ideas and remarkable talent for narration which characterise the creations of this world-famous author". He was the first English-language recipient. At the award ceremony in Switzerland, Carl David af Wirsén praised Kipling and the English literary tradition:

> The Swedish Academy, in awarding the Nobel Prize in Literature this year to Rudyard Kipling, desires to pay a tribute to the literature of England, so rich in manifold glories, and to the greatest genius in the realm of narrative that that country has produced in our times.

Following this achievement, Kipling published Rewards and Fairies, which contained If, voted Britain's favourite poem in a BBC opinion poll in 1995. He turned down several recommendations for knighthood and was considered for Poet Laureate, though this position was never offered to him.

The sense of perseverance, honour and stoicism in If prevailed in many of his opinions, including that on the First World War. Writing in The New Army in Training in 1915, he scorned those who refused conscription, considering

> ....what will be the position in years to come of the young man who has deliberately elected to outcaste himself from this all-embracing brotherhood? What of his family, and, above all, what of his descendants, when the books have been closed and the last balance struck of sacrifice and sorrow in every hamlet, village, parish, suburb, city, shire, district, province, and Dominion throughout the Empire?

This attitude saw him encourage his son, John, to go to war, and he was promptly killed at the Battle of Loos in September 1915, aged 18. Last seen during the battle stumbling blindly through the mud, screaming in agony after an exploding shell had ripped his face apart, Kipling would write—

"If any question why we died
Tell them, because our fathers lied"

—perhaps betraying the guilt he felt at encouraging his son to go to war and finding him a position in the Irish Guards through his friendship with commander-in-chief Lord Roberts, for whom he had established The Friend in Bloemfontein. His death inspired much of Kipling's successive writing, notably My Boy Jack and a two-volume history of the Irish Guards, considered one of the finest examples of regimental history. Ironically, though his writing and his political position had arguably cost John his life, after the war he became friends with a French soldier whose copy of Kim, kept in his breast pocket, had stopped a bullet and saved his life. For a while the book and the soldier's Croix de Guerre were with Kipling, presented as tokens of gratitude, and they remained in contact, though when Kipling learned of the soldier's child he insisted on returning both book and medal.

He kept writing until 1930, though at a considerably slower pace, and to less success. His death, already once incorrectly announced early by a magazine in a premature obituary (and to which he responded "I've just read that I am dead. Don't forget to delete me from your list of subscribers") came on 18th January 1936, at the age of 70, from a perforated duodenal ulcer. His coffin was carried by, among others, his cousin the Prime Minister Stanley Baldwin, and his marble casket covered by a Union flag. He was cremated at Golders Green Crematorium in Northwest London and his ashes are buried at Poets' Corner in Westminster Abbey, alongside the graves of both Charles Dickens and Thomas Hardy.

In conjunction with various earthly memorials which commemorate him, alongside his extensive writing, he has a crater on Mercury named after him. The question of memorial and monument is much-addressed in English Literature and, as various great authors and poets have agreed before Kipling's time, his memory lives on more vivaciously set in his words, far longer and better represented than it could set in stone.

Rudyard Kipling - A Concise Bibliography

Books
The City of Dreadful Night (1885, short story)
Plain Tales from the Hills (1888)
Soldiers Three (1888)
The Story of the Gadsbys (1888)
In Black and White (1888)
Under the Deodars (1888)
The Phantom 'Rickshaw and other Eerie Tales (1888)
Wee Willie Winkie and Other Child Stories (1888)
Life's Handicap (1891)
The Light that Failed (1891) (novel)
American Notes (1891) (non-fiction)
The Naulahka: A Story of West and East (1892) (with Wolcott Balestie)
Many Inventions (1893)
The Jungle Book (1894)
Mowgli's Brothers (short story)
Kaa's Hunting (short story)
Tiger! Tiger! (short story)
The White Seal (short story)
Rikki-Tikki-Tavi (short story)
Toomai of the Elephants (short story)
Her Majesty's Servants (originally titled Servants of the Queen) (short story)

The Second Jungle Book (1895)
How Fear Came (short story)
The Miracle of Purun Bhagat (short story)
Letting in the Jungle (short story)
The Undertakers (short story)
The King's Ankus (short story)
Quiquern (short story)
Red Dog" (short story)
The Spring Running (short story)
Captains Courageous (1896) (novel)
The Day's Work (1898)
A Fleet in Being (1898)
Stalky & Co. (1899)
From Sea to Sea and Other Sketches, Letters of Travel (1899) (non-fiction)
Kim (1901) (novel)
Just So Stories for Little Children (1902)
Traffics and Discoveries (1904) (24 collected short stories)
With the Night Mail (1905) A Story of 2000 A.D
Puck of Pook's Hill (1906)
The Brushwood Boy (1907)
Actions and Reactions (1909)
A Song of the English (1909) (with W. Heath Robinson illustrator)
Rewards and Fairies (1910)
A History of England (1911) (non-fiction with Charles Robert Leslie Fletcher)
Songs from Books (1912)
As Easy as A.B.C. (1912) (Science-fiction short story)
The Fringes of the Fleet (1915) (non-fiction)
Sea Warfare (1916) (non-fiction)
A Diversity of Creatures (1917)
Land and Sea Tales for Scouts and Guides (1923)
The Irish Guards in the Great War (1923) (non-fiction)
Debits and Credits (1926)
A Book of Words (1928) (non-fiction)
Thy Servant a Dog (1930)
Limits and Renewals (1932)
Tales of India: the Windermere Series (1935)
Something of Myself (1937) (autobiography)
The Elephant's Child (fiction)

Autobiographies and Speeches
A Book of Words (1928)
Something of Myself (1937)

Short Story Collections
Quartette (1885) – with his father, mother, and sister
Plain Tales from the Hills (1888)

Soldiers Three, The Story of the Gadsbys, In Black and White (1888)
The Phantom 'Rickshaw and other Eerie Tales (1888)
Under the Deodars (1888)
Wee Willie Winkie and Other Child Stories (1888)
Life's Handicap (1891)
Many Inventions (1893)
The Jungle Book (1894)
The Second Jungle Book (1895)
The Day's Work (1898)
Life's Handicap (1899)
Stalky & Co. (1899)
Just So Stories (1902)
Traffics and Discoveries (1904)
Puck of Pook's Hill (1906)
Actions and Reactions (1909)
Abaft the Funnel (1909)
Rewards and Fairies (1910)
The Eyes of Asia (1917)
A Diversity of Creatures (1917)
Land and Sea Tales for Scouts and Guides (1923)
Debits and Credits (1926)
Thy Servant a Dog (1930)
Limits and Renewals (1932)

Military Collections
A Fleet in Being (1898)
France at War (1915)
The New Army in Training (1915)
Sea Warfare (1916)
The War in the Mountains (1917)
The Graves of the Fallen (1919)
The Irish Guards in the Great War (1923)

Poetry Collections
Schoolboy Lyrics (1881)
Echoes (1884) – with his sister, Alice ('Trix')
Departmental Ditties (1886)
Barrack-Room Ballads (1890)
The Seven Seas (1896)
An Almanac of Twelve Sports (1898, with illustrations by William Nicholson)
The Five Nations (1903)
Collected Verse (1907)
Songs from Books (1912)
The Years Between (1919)
Rudyard Kipling's Verse: Definitive Edition (1940)
The Muse Among the Motors (poetry)

In addition Kipling wrote and published many hundreds of poems too numerous to include here